YOUR BABY IS NOT A DOLL

Tips For The First-Time Parent

SHAYLA M. FORT, RN, MSN, RNC-MNN, CLC

This book is not intended as a substitute for any medical advice received from a professional healthcare provider. All efforts have been made to ensure that the information shared within this book was correct at the time of publication. The author and publisher do not assume and hereby disclaim any liability to any party for any loss, damage, or disruption caused by errors or omissions, whether such errors or omissions result from negligence, accident, or any other cause. Please speak with your healthcare provider prior to making any final decisions about your plan of care.

Copyright ©2024 Shayla M. Fort

All rights reserved, including the right to reproduce this book
in whole or portions thereof in any form whatsoever.

print ISBN: 979-8-35096-981-8
ebook ISBN: 979-8-35096-982-5

CONTENTS

Preface	1
Terms and Definitions	7
Chapter 1. **We Are Pregnant!**	11
Chapter 2. **Grandparents with Good Intentions**	17
Chapter 3. **Reliable Resources**	21
Chapter 4. **Choosing a Pediatrician**	27
Chapter 5. **Vaccines and Medications at Birth**	31
Chapter 6. **Hospital Tour**	35
Chapter 7. **Breastfeeding**	39
Chapter 8. **Formula Feeding**	43
Chapter 9. **CPR**	47
Chapter 10. **Safe Registry**	51
Chapter 11. **Car Seats**	55
Chapter 12. **Advocacy**	59
Chapter 13. **You've Delivered! How Do You Feel?**	63
Chapter 14. **Wait! My Baby Is a Doll**	69

PREFACE

The newborn stage of life is undoubtedly one of the most vulnerable and innocent times in a person's life. You were born and now things are happening to you by people that you cannot see and voices that you have never heard. Babies are some of the most trusting beings, whether they want to or not. They depend solely on us to hold, feed, and care for them in every way. What other choice do they have?

Well, that's where we, as parents, come in. We have the choice to do what is best for our babies. As first-time parents who have no experience with babies, have never had a baby, and so many people around you are telling you what is best for YOUR baby, how do we know what's best? This space of the unknown brings about a sense of vulnerability for you as well. At birth, we are handed this baby that we only know from the images on the ultrasound, movements in your womb, or hearing its heartbeat. Now you have to care for them for the rest of your life.

Self-help books generally want to help the reader solve a problem for themselves. This book is geared toward helping both the expectant parent and the newborn. As a nurse, your primary responsibility to your patients is their safety. As it turns out, safety is the primary responsibility of a parent. Safety for an expectant parent begins with realizing that you are not alone in your thoughts of, *What do I do with this baby?* or not knowing what you don't know. There is no rule book to parenting; however, there are some things that you should know about as a parent relating to your child's health and well-being. This book is going to give insight from the perspective of a mother who is a professional registered nurse with experience in maternal/newborn health. Let's turn your "I didn't think of that" into "Yes, that has been taken care of." Before we get down to it, let's lay a little foundation, shall we?

Having a baby is one of the most precious gifts and life-changing occasions in a person's life. As a mother/baby nurse, my mission was to set new families on a firm foundation as they embarked on this journey called parenthood. My passion was to do whatever was in my power to make this new normal a smooth transition. The goal was to help new and experienced parents feel encouraged and more prepared to care for themselves and the beginning stages of this precious new life.

This reality can carry many emotions—excitement, anxiety, and even fear. Excited parents are often in glee over the new nursery, matching outfits for the hospital stay, and even the clothes the baby will wear home. One day, a patient assigned to me had a small suitcase in her room dedicated to the numerous outfits planned for her new baby girl. Most of them still had the tags on them. The funny thing about this is that the car seat was nowhere to be found. The father was making a trip to the local Target to get one. When asked about the vaccines ordered for her baby, there was minimal knowledge. In fact, during the postpartum phase, it was her first time to learn basic care practices for her new baby. Her demeanor became fearful and anxiety-stricken. This mother's situation, unfortunately, was not unique.

It is the goal of this book to help develop a new emotion—calm. Calm will come from a new awareness of subjects that most first-timers may not know about and how to handle those who believe they know it all when it comes to babies. A perfect time nor a perfect method for preparing for a newborn has yet to be discovered. The first time that I began to consider what to prepare for when expecting a baby was when my best friend told me that she was pregnant. As a mother/baby nurse, I knew that I would be called upon for help. I outlined a checklist for her to follow. It looked a little something like this.

Pre-baby Checklist

✓ **Hospital Tour**

- Helps to decrease feeling overwhelmed in an unfamiliar space at the time of labor and delivery

✓ **Perinatal Classes**

- **Check on the classes offered at the hospital. Some are even free!**

    - Infant CPR

    - Childbirth

    - Breastfeeding

✓ **Pediatrician**

- Select a pediatrician that suits your healthcare desires

✓ **Gift Registries**

- Create at least two gift registries after you reach twenty-four weeks

✓ **Hospital Packing**

- Pack an overnight hospital bag by thirty-four weeks

- Only pack essential items

- Hygiene products
- Flip-flops or slippers
- Baby Blanket
- Going home outfit for baby
- Pajamas

✓ **Baby Proofing**

- Baby-proof (electrical sockets, cushion the sharp edges on furniture)
- Add locks to cabinets for anything that could be poisonous if consumed, e.g., cleaning products
- Don't wash all clothes until you know the size of the baby

This checklist is derived from my nursing experiences with patients, gaps in patient knowledge, and basic nursing knowledge. Once I became a mother, I was able to witness firsthand parental necessities that I didn't even consider before becoming one. Now that I am a nurse educator, there are some new subjects that I would add. These subjects will be addressed further throughout this book. As the author, it is my hope that this book will shed light on what I believe are the essentials to preparing for a baby, besides clothing. Your baby is precious and beautiful; this is true. However, the fact of the matter is that "your baby is not a doll."

TERMS AND DEFINITIONS

AAP (American Academy of Pediatrics) – an organization of pediatricians committed to "optimal physical, mental, and social health and well-being for all infants, children, adolescents, and young adults."

ADA (American Diabetes Association) – an association that strives to improve the lives of people living with diabetes as well as spread awareness of the disease.

AHA (American Heart Association) – an association dedicated to spreading awareness of heart disease and developing ways for lay people to save lives.

AWHONN (The Association for Women's Health, Obstetrics, and Neonatal Nurses) – an association that is committed to supporting nurses with a vision to make a difference in the lives of women and newborns.

Baby Blues – general feeling of sadness for a few days after delivering a baby.

Breastfeeding – the practice of using breasts to produce human milk for newborns. This milk can also be pumped and fed to a baby through a bottle.

CBC (Complete Blood Count) – a common lab test ordered by medical providers to examine contents of blood.

CPR (Cardiopulmonary Resuscitation) – emergency practice for providing ventilation and compression efforts to improve blood circulation and restart heart function.

Formula Feeding – the practice of feeding a baby with an ultra-processed food designed for children up to one year of age. May come in liquid or powdered forms.

OBGYN (Obstetrics and Gynecology) – refers to a medical professional that specializes in obstetrics and gynecology.

Pediatrician – a medical provider that specializes in the healthcare of infants, children, and adolescents.

Perinatal – time period immediately before and after birth

Pinterest – an app available on smart phones, iPads, and computers that allows visual interpretation of ideas in just about any category that you could imagine.

Postpartum Depression – a form of depression that can occur after the delivery of a baby and carries many faces, including an intense form of sadness that can lead to an inability to enjoy the new baby.

Postpartum Psychosis – is the severest form of postpartum depression. It is a mental illness where the birthing person becomes detached from reality, experiences delusions, and experiences paranoia.

CHAPTER 1

WE ARE PREGNANT!

"The test was positive!" "We're having a baby!" "I'm going to be a mom!" "I'm going to be a dad!" These are all common statements often heard in early pregnancy. What was your first phrase? For me, when my husband and I found out we were pregnant, I remember hugging and staring at each other and thinking, *What now?* The very next step to take is to schedule an appointment with your obstetric provider. This is critical because this first appointment confirms the positive home pregnancy test and begins the first steps for your prenatal care.

During this first or second appointment, you can expect laboratory blood work, a request for a urine sample, and a collection of your health history. This may feel invasive, but know that each request serves a purpose.

The purpose is to create a baseline of your current health needs for your pregnancy. One of the labs is called a CBC. A CBC reveals the status of your blood components that can affect your pregnancy. A low blood count, for example, can lead to fainting spells, weakness, and tiredness. Knowing this information will prompt your provider to take the necessary steps in your treatment plan to improve these results. Some steps may include changes to your diet or prescribing medications.

During this time, the nurse or provider will also provide you with literature on what to expect from month to month. No one expects that you will retain this information in one sitting, but we highly encourage you to read it at your leisure. We understand that this can be an overwhelming appointment. Your appointment may wrap up with the provider asking, "Do you have any questions?" Well, duh! Of course, you do. You just may not know when or how to ask. My advice is to ask any and every question you can think of at any time during your pregnancy. If your provider has a patient portal service, use it. It is a great way to get some of your questions answered in between appointments. Please note that the responses may be from the provider's nurse and not the provider. No need to doubt their response; it is based on experience and in collaboration with your provider. Additionally, reading the literature given to you at your appointment will answer some of those questions quite often.

If you have not already done so, your next stop after leaving the provider's office is the pharmacy to pick up a bottle of over-the-counter prenatal vitamins. Most insurance plans cover the cost of prenatal vitamins, so you can also request a prescription from the provider. I used to think this was crazy, seeing as though prenatal vitamins typically aren't that expensive. However, after spending some time working in an OB/GYN office, I soon learned that your cost could go anywhere from $20 for an over-the-counter bottle to $5 for a prescription bottle. That is $15 in savings that can go toward other expenses.

Prenatal vitamins are highly important for your baby's development. Prenatal vitamins help support the growth of the baby and also sustain your health. In my practice, I have heard women state that they don't like to take prenatal vitamins because they make them feel sick. This could be due to several circumstances, as discussed below.

Timing – Due to the high concentration of supplements, taking prenatal vitamins on an empty stomach can cause stomach upset. If you are not accustomed to eating breakfast, this could further upset your stomach when taking prenatal vitamins in the morning. Oftentimes, it is more tolerable when taken at night.

Medication - If you take other medications, consider taking the prenatal vitamin at least two hours after the other medication. For instance, if you require blood pressure medications that you take in the morning, take the prenatal vitamin at night. If your other medications are taken multiple times a day, a general recommendation is to take the prenatal vitamin at least an hour apart from them, unless otherwise stated by your provider.

Swallowing Ability – Even as adults, the ability to swallow large pills can be a challenge. If this person is you, consider switching your prenatal vitamin over to gummies. They contain the same volume of ingredients that the pill form contains. Be sure to read your labels. If your provider prescribes a specific type of prenatal vitamin that only comes in pill form, ask if the pill can be crushed. This way, the pill can be mixed and ingested with foods such as applesauce or pudding. Your baby needs this. You must find which prenatal vitamin option works for you. What is not an option is going without one.

Depending on how you got here on your journey to parenthood, deciding when to tell family and friends may differ from person to person. Those who spontaneously conceived may be eager to share the good news. Others who require assistance with conception or have experienced a previous loss may decide to wait a little longer. Remember that you are not on anyone else's schedule to share. This is a precious moment in your life that you can cherish between you and your partner for as long as you deem necessary. Or at least until your baby reveals itself through the bump in your belly. Know that whichever decision you make is what is best for you and your growing family.

If you have shared the news or decided to wait to share it, be prepared to be smothered with advice. Much of which will be outdated or simply incorrect. Two of the most incorrect pieces of advice I have heard both professionally and personally are regarding infant safe sleep and breastfeeding, which I will get into later. They all have the best intentions for you and your baby, but keep in mind that their advice mostly stems from their experience and opinions, not facts. Congratulations on your pregnancy! Now who do we share the news with first?

CHAPTER 2

GRANDPARENTS WITH GOOD INTENTIONS

When revealing your pregnancy news, the grandparents are typically among the first to know. Why is that? Is it because they are the ones to whom you tell all of your important news first? Is it because they will be the ones assisting with the baby's care? Regardless of the reason, you chose to make them the first to know. With the evolution of social media, the creativity of sharing pregnancy news is remarkable. Taking pictures and saying "I'm pregnant" instead of saying cheese. I gave my parents and in-laws a T-shirt that read, *Promoted to Grandma and Grandpa.* The list could go on and on. Nevertheless, one thing is clear: the day that they have been waiting for is here. If your parents are only living in your heart, do not worry; those aunts, uncles, and besties will serve in this role for those ready to impart their good-intentioned advice to you.

Whether you were raised by your biological parents or adopted as a baby, unsolicited advice may begin innocently by sharing a story of your pregnancy or your first days, including any diagnosis received, cravings, and maternity clothes worn. They may even go grab the family photo albums, reminiscing over your newborn pictures. Part of this excitement may be a list of *dos* and *don'ts*. These *dos* and *don'ts* are also known as old wives' tales or advice. I recall one of the *don'ts* from my mother when I was pregnant with my son, which was that I could not reach high above my head because I could wrap the umbilical cord around my baby's neck. I thought this was a bit absurd, so when I asked my provider, he informed me that this was indeed an old wives' tale. Another old wives' tale that my mom shared with me was that if you place an uncooked egg at the top of the doorframe of the room the baby is in the most, it helps to decrease crying during teething. I later found that the list of old wives' tales is extensive, impacting both the birthing person and the baby. We have to give them a break, though. If something worked for Great-Grandmama, Grandmama, and your mom, why wouldn't it work for you too, *right*? Their intentions are great and are there because, although you are pregnant with their grandchild, you are still *their* baby.

YOUR BABY IS NOT A DOLL

When in the delivery room, it is amazing how many birthing people call out for their moms, whether their partner is present or not. I did not remember doing so; however, my husband told me that I asked for my mom as well. Giving birth yields a great deal of vulnerability, much as when we were babies, so it's only natural that we would want our parents to be there to make it all right. If you have the type of parent that can become overwhelming to have around in emotionally driven situations, try working out a game plan for the role you prefer them to play. For instance, if you prefer presence instead of talking, make your desires known to all whom you wish to be a part of the birthing process.

One of the great pieces of advice that is shared quite often is to get some rest. The rest you need now is for you, as your body is working hard to grow and develop a new life. Nevertheless, when people say rest up for the baby, can someone please tell me who has ever rested for something due to occur months later? I repeat, this rest is for you now. In an attempt to gain some rest, pregnancy will not always make this as easy of a process as it once was. This is where pillows become your best friend. Many companies have come up with pregnancy pillows to help you rest more comfortably. It is recommended to purchase one as soon as possible to be ready for the day you wake up with your bump. Partners don't often like these pillows as they do take up a great bit of bed space; however, most great partners understand this minor inconvenience. What your partner should be more concerned about is the constant repositioning, the multiple bathroom trips throughout the night that may keep them up and the resentment of their peaceful sleep.

When you see a grandparent come across your phone or show up at your door, answer it and let them in because, throughout the wealth of information that they will share with you, there is a precious gem in there that will soon be known as "words of wisdom." The next question is, while parents and grandparents alike will be ready to unload their knowledge on pregnancy, birth, and later parenting, how do you decipher what is a fact and what is an opinion?

CHAPTER 3

RELIABLE RESOURCES

For as long as I can remember, my source of truth has come from two places. Bible stories and my momma's stories. As a believer in the Christian faith, I believe the Word of God is truth. As a momma's girl, I believed the word of my mother was truth. As it relates to pregnancy and birth, I developed my truth from my experiences as a mother/baby nurse. As an expectant mother, my beliefs on raising my son were guided by my upbringing, my husband's upbringing, and things we both would have changed between the two. At the end of the day, we are just trying to do our best.

Needless to say, if you are having a baby, advice is coming. Now is the time to explore the idea of who and what makes a reliable resource.

At my wedding, we decided to have an advice table at our reception. It not only gave our guests something to do during the cocktail hour, but my husband and I were able to hear some wisdom from those who had traveled the road of marriage before us. The same goes for new babies. I have even started to see advice tables being done at baby showers; however, they are written on diapers to keep it cute. Now that you are having a baby, whoever that person was for you while you were growing up is going to give you more information about pregnancy and babies than you could ever ask. Unfortunately, the problem with most of this information is that it comes from a place that may have family traditions, such as this is how *I did it*, how *your grandmother did it,* and how your *great-grandmother did it, too*! Any rebellion against these family traditions could cause negative feelings, as if you were saying that what they have done for years before you were wrong. It may have been, but they don't have to know that.

What they can know is that new research has been conducted since their time as a new parent, proving how some of those practices can and should be tweaked a bit. For example, recommendations from the past used to say to let your infant sleep on their stomach. We now know that lying on the back to sleep is the better way to decrease the rates of sudden infant death syndrome. This has to do with evidence-based research that tells us that when infants sleep in the prone position, it causes an unalignment with the functionality of vital organ systems necessary to fight stressors, such as the ability to breathe, resulting in the cessation of normal blood flow, leading to death. Please understand that the recommendations given by your healthcare provider are only done after evidence-based research has been completed to support the practice.

If your hospital is not participating in the best evidence-based practices, switch hospitals and providers if necessary. Science will never be perfect—nothing is—but it does its best to supply the consumer with the best information to help you make an informed decision. With that being said, sometimes the phrase "If it ain't broke, don't fix it" just doesn't apply. Keeping everything the same keeps us stagnant and not progressive in our care for these little ones.

Outside of immediate family, there will be countless other means of information available to you, both unsolicited and solicited. The key is to determine which is a reliable source of information and which sources I should take with a grain of salt. Here are some tips for doing so when it comes to healthcare:

Healthcare information should be sought first through your medical providers and nurses. Nowadays, most offices have patient portal systems that allow patients to submit questions that arise outside of their appointments. Take advantage of this service. It will help alleviate some anxiety. If you don't like the provider's advice, never be afraid to ask for a second opinion from another reputable medical provider.

Dr. Google will lead you down any path that you want to take. If you are looking for something to confirm your thoughts, you will find it. If you are looking for something to dispute your thoughts, you will find that, too. It doesn't make either of them factual. If you are going to search online, do so on reputable sites such as the American Academy of Pediatrics, the Association of Women's Obstetric and Neonatal Nurses, the American Heart Association, the American Diabetes Association, or the Center for Disease Control. All the aforementioned sites are reputable because they have been founded on producing evidence-based guidelines for their standards and healthcare promotions. It is important to note that healthcare providers use these organizations' standards of care and their experiences to map out their plans of care.

Now that we have discussed reputable online resources, is there a reputable person or group of people that you know that you should depend on as a reliable source? You. The answer is you. You are your most reliable resource. We all want to help each other, and we all, deep down, want the help that is being offered. Nevertheless, you only know what is truly helpful to YOU. You know what is best for you and your new baby. It is important, as a new parent, that you trust and believe that you have insight as well. Advice is needed and appreciated, but final decisions should be based on what you choose is best for you and your new baby. One of those choices is the care of the infant after discharge.

CHAPTER 4

CHOOSING A PEDIATRICIAN

Whenever a person is admitted to the hospital, regardless of the reason, the goal is to get discharged. A patient's plan of care will be aligned with how to care for yourself as quickly as possible and get you back into a normal life. For a birthing person or baby, a part of this discharge planning on admission is learning who you have chosen to be your pediatrician. This information is requested for a few highly important reasons. One of those reasons is for lab results. From the moment your baby is born, data is collected to help understand their transition to life outside of the womb as well as to determine a treatment plan for the hospital staff and beyond. This data will include weight, length, head circumference, blood type if the birthing person has a negative blood type, and a general assessment. All test results are sent to your chosen pediatrician to maintain records to guide them on the baby's trends in development over the next few months and the next several years. Typically, the pediatrician will want to see the baby for their first office visit within two to three days after discharge. This appointment follows any pending results, concerns, or general check-ups.

One day, while admitting a patient, I asked her who she had chosen for her pediatrician. She looked at me and said, "People do that before the baby is even here?" It was at that point that I decided that expectant parents needed to know that yes, that is a thing. Planning for the needs of your baby, especially their health, is precisely why your baby is not a doll. They need someone to maintain records and guide them on their journey to a healthy life through regular assessments. These ongoing assessments help understand the baby's trends in development. Additionally, it reduces trips to the ER and sitting for three hours just to be told that your baby has an ear infection.

Choosing a pediatrician has changed so much over the years. When I asked my mother about how she chose my pediatrician, the answer was simply a doctor who her friend used for their kids.

This is a typical starting point for any new parent. It is pretty common to use a provider known to someone you trust. While this is a typical starting point, I would not advise stopping there. Consider looking into that provider and finding out what their practices are on vaccination, breastfeeding, or whatever else is important to you for your baby.

Most offices even now have the option for you to meet directly with your pediatrician candidate to address your questions and tour the office. I was so excited when the provider we were interested in had this option. This allowed us to gain answers to any looming questions before selecting them. Additionally, you are allowed to check out the personality of the provider. Do they rush? Are they willing to answer your questions? How did they make you feel? Is this person a good fit for your baby and your family? If not, keep searching. If you are like my patient and are now in the postpartum phase of pregnancy, know that most hospitals can provide you with a list of pediatricians for you to choose from.

Looking through a list of pediatricians may feel overwhelming with the other tasks for the baby, but it is an essential one. Here are a few tips for tackling this list in your search:

1. *Location*: Mark out all of the locations that are not feasible for commuting from your home.

2. *Demographics*: Do you have a preference for gender, race, or ethnicity? This may take a bit longer as you search for the person on their office website or

on Google. Once you find them, mark them out as appropriate for you.

3. *Medical Management*: Do you plan to vaccinate or not vaccinate your baby? Unless it specifically states the office's position on vaccinations, you may need to contact them directly and eliminate them where applicable.

4. *Availability*: Now that you have shortened your list, start calling to see if they are accepting new patients. Not accepting new patients is a common problem faced by parents who are choosing a pediatrician post-birth. This may feel stressful, but don't worry; it will work itself out. You can always change later if need be.

5. *Insurance Coverage*: Healthcare coverage is not created equal, and every provider does not accept the same coverage. Be prepared for this when asked by the office before setting an appointment. Once you have a match, lock in that appointment.

With all of this planning, one thing that you may not have started to consider is vaccinations. Have you thought about it? Have you done any research on the topic yet? If so, have you and your partner discussed where you stand on the issue? Let's talk about it.

CHAPTER 5

VACCINES AND MEDICATIONS AT BIRTH

Vaccinations are often a hot topic of conversation in many different settings and groups of people. Unfortunately, we often get our information from incorrect settings and groups of people. Social media has grown into a platform that allows individuals of all ages, backgrounds, and differing levels of expertise to express their thoughts and opinions. With some creativity and crafty editing, this information may be delivered in a way that draws a following of people who believe whatever is being said. To make matters even more interesting, this information is given within thirty-second increments and stated with such confidence that it is mistaken for truth. Now don't get me wrong; I have learned a lot from various social media influencers on helpful decorating tips, DIY projects, and recipes, to name a few; however, for health information, I reserve it for medical professionals. What I appreciate about the medical and nursing professions is their ability to adapt to social changes and relay health information. Some medical professionals are using social media platforms to reach those who use this tool to guide their decisions on different aspects of their lives. It offers the opportunity for facts to be passed along, not opinions.

As a nurse, vaccinations and medications at birth can be answered by simply considering risks versus benefits. Vaccinations were created to eradicate diseases with a high probability of death or severe illness if contracted. A few years ago, an article came out stating that vaccinations were a leading cause of autism in children. Autism, or autism spectrum disorder, is defined by autismspeaks.org as a broad range of conditions characterized by challenges with social skills, repetitive behaviors, speech, and nonverbal communication. Which vaccine, and was it due to administration at a certain time versus another? How do we account for the children who are autistic and were not vaccinated?

The lack of support for this conclusion and lack of answers to questions, such as the ones I posed, is more than likely why that article was later determined to be unfounded. Pregnancy is a journey with many twists and turns, and we could consider many other factors that could lead to a diagnosis of autism. Let's keep in mind the risks versus benefits discussion. If autism is your concern, is that risk worth the benefit of having a child who is alive? Autism is not the only concern with vaccinations that has been voiced. There are also concerns over preservatives and the schedule of administration. The good news is that some vaccinations come with a preservative-free option.

The schedule of administration was a minor concern for me as a parent. According to the Center for Disease Control's (CDC), most current recommendations consist of seventeen vaccinations, including COVID-19, for children and adolescents scheduled from birth until eighteen years of age. Note that these vaccinations may come in multiple doses. At birth, the newborn is offered two medications, vitamin K (Phytonadione) injection and erythromycin eye ointment, and one vaccination, Hepatitis B.

Vitamin K is the medication responsible for assisting the blood to clot. Babies are born with very little vitamin K of their own due to low bacteria found in their intestine at birth, which is where good bacteria are formed. Without it, the baby is susceptible to uncontrollable bleeding if a cut or fall occurs. A lot of accidents can happen during that time, and I appreciate any protection my newborn baby can get. It is given to the baby's thigh with minimal pain. Not to mention, if you have a boy and are interested in having him circumcised, please be aware that one of the qualifications for most hospitals is that the baby has received vitamin K. If not, expect a no to that procedure request. Keep in mind that while patients have the right to refuse treatment, providers also reserve the right to refuse to perform elective procedures for safety reasons. Erythromycin ointment is applied to both eyes for the prevention of infection that can be transmitted when moving through the birth canal. Administration of erythromycin is fairly simple, pain-free, and has little or no side effects.

If the decision to vaccinate your baby is unclear, it is highly encouraged that you speak with your pediatrician before making any final decisions. In the previous chapter, we discussed choosing a pediatrician. This is one of those questions for you to ask during that meeting. In some cases, the choice of pediatrician may be decided for you as some pediatricians will not accept you as a patient if you decline to vaccinate. No worries, though. There are some pediatricians around who will support that decision. You just have to work a little harder to find them.

CHAPTER 6

HOSPITAL TOUR

If you are planning to deliver in a hospital, the facility was quite possibly chosen by where your medical team has privileges and not so much about what you know about the facility. Unless you work in the women's center of a hospital, it is safe to say that for most expectant parents, the first time you will see what your labor and delivery room and recovery room in mother/baby or postpartum will look like will be at the time of delivery. Today, facilities are providing that opportunity sooner through hospital tours. Unfortunately, finding out this information may take some initiative on the part of the expectant parent to contact the facility and ask if they offer one. This will typically lead you to a website where more information may be provided on the services offered by the facility.

While working at a hospital in my hometown, I would see groups of expectant parents coming around the unit with a guide to tour the facility. I later became one of those tour guides. During that experience, I learned that the value of touring the facility where you are going to deliver your baby carries much more than just the tour itself. For the baby, it provides immunity properties as the birthing person touches various surfaces in the facility, building antibodies for the newborn upon their arrival. For the expectant parents, it reduces anxieties about what to expect upon their arrival. For the staff, awareness of the education being provided to future patients on what the hospital will provide for you and what items you should pack.

This also helps to avoid packing inappropriately for the hospital setting, such as bringing open-flame candles. Open flamed candles are a danger to us all, and nurses like myself will blow them out.

Hospital tours also carry the benefit of talking with other expectant parents and hearing the answers to other questions that you may or may not have thought to ask but are glad you now know. Additionally, you have the opportunity to learn more about the facility through things such as:

- Parking location and fees

- Location of the cafeteria

  - Are partner meals included in patient meals?

- Visitation Policy

- Supplies provided by the facility

For those who are looking for specific characteristics of the hospital, such as diversity in staff or breastfeeding support, a hospital tour is a prime opportunity to see and discuss those things firsthand with someone who works on that unit. Lastly, you get the opportunity to see the rooms while beginning to picture yourself there as you are nearing the end of your pregnancy. If your hospital is anything like mine, you get a gift afterward! Who doesn't like free stuff??!! If you have the time, don't skip the tour. It will be worth your time.

CHAPTER 7

BREASTFEEDING

Breastfeeding—to do or not to do—has always been the question. Some women may decide to breastfeed based on what the mothers in their families did. This decision may also be influenced by horror stories from friends and families about their own experiences. Another reason may be due to some sort of past trauma where the woman may not want her breasts touched at all.

When I became a nurse, my first position was on a unit called High-Risk Obstetrics. This is a floor that a patient may be admitted to when complications with the pregnancy arise, such as preterm labor, hyperemesis gravidarum, or uncontrolled comorbidities that are affecting the pregnancy. Oftentimes, due to some of these diagnoses requiring admission until delivery, the patient would return to the same room after delivery. A rapport was developed with those nurses, and from a hospital standpoint, it was less costly to turn over the room, otherwise known as cleaning it. It was kind of a win-win for both sides. Because we didn't have to care for the baby once it was delivered, it was typical that we didn't place that much attention on breastfeeding. That was the job of the nursery nurse.

Breast pumps were set up and encouraged to be used, but from my experience, if you used them, great; if you didn't, no problem. I would hear colleagues suggest just giving the baby a bottle when challenges arose. After a couple of years, I transferred to the mother/baby unit. We had wonderful educators who taught us how to follow baby-friendly guidelines, which included how to support breastfeeding mothers on their breastfeeding goals even though we were not a baby-friendly facility at the time. The turning point for me in understanding the big picture of breastfeeding was when I was offered the opportunity to obtain certification as a lactation counselor. While it didn't mean that much to me when it was offered, it seemed like a great opportunity to grow in my career.

When I returned to work after completing the course, my very first patient was exclusively breastfeeding and was having some challenges. My mind was so fresh with the knowledge that I just acquired that I just spilled it all over her and soon did her milk supply. She was so excited to show me how much she pumped after each session and how well the baby had improved with latching. Breastfeeding is more than just a means to feed your baby. It can be a bonding experience. Additionally, breastmilk has been coined the title "liquid gold" because of its highly nutritional properties that no manmade formula has yet to touch, making it in some cases a nutritional necessity.

Historically, the values of breastmilk were shown during the times of slavery, when slaves were forced to breastfeed the babies of the master's children, often leaving nothing for their babies. This liquid gold carries healing measures. A mother with exposure to addictive substances can help their babies dealing with withdrawal symptoms by breastfeeding or breastmilk-feeding their newborn carrying tiny traces that pass through the breastmilk. Some may say, "Why would you want to give the baby more drugs?" If you have ever seen a baby going through withdrawal, you know that withdrawal symptoms have been lessened when small traces from the recovering mother are passed to the recovering newborn baby.

Newborns that are born prematurely have a greater chance of improving their growth and medical issues from being premature when they are given breastmilk. Crazy enough, I even had a friend who claimed that when she had pink eyes, she rubbed a little breastmilk on her eye, and it began to heal. Coincidence or not, it encouraged her to continue breastfeeding to be sure her baby received the one gift only she could give.

I have had the pleasure of helping many mothers achieve their breastfeeding goals, both great and small. For those who decide that breastfeeding is not the choice they make for their newborn, we discuss ways to dry her milk as well as the steps to properly mix formula, which we will get into in the next chapter. If you are questioning the decision to breastfeed your newborn, be prepared for both negative and positive advice. During your hospital tour, ask the tour guide about baby-friendly practices and if they have a lactation consultant in-house. Understand that some challenges may arise, but with the help of a trained nurse or lactation consultant, you can persevere through those challenges. The decision to breastfeed or not should be an informed one. The answer to this question is a personal one, and there is nothing to be ashamed of if you find that, despite the lecture we give you, breastfeeding is just not for you, and that is okay!

CHAPTER 8

FORMULA FEEDING

Formula feeding is an alternative option for providing nourishment to your baby. They come in several different variations: regular, sensitive, organic, and soy, just to name a few. There are even specialized formulas suited for babies with special nutritional needs. Your initial encounter with the formula for your use can vary as well. Some may first meet formula while in the hospital, while others may have received samples from their doctor's office or in the mail. When I was pregnant with my son, my birth plan included exclusively breastfeeding; however, before I stepped foot into the hospital for delivery, there were already samples being delivered to my home. I often wondered how the formula companies received my information. That part was never really made clear. Nevertheless, I decided to keep it as a backup just in case of emergencies. After all, as a mother/baby nurse, I have seen how, even with the most determined mother, breastfeeding is not an easy task.

Hospitals typically only supply one manufacturer for formula. Often, this one manufacturer will source a few variations to the type of formula that can be offered to your baby. Some parents may choose to formula feed for many different reasons, including a lack of desire to breastfeed, a low breastmilk supply, difficulty achieving an effective latch, or a medical necessity. Historically, formulas were designed to mimic the nutrients in breastmilk and were introduced to provide nutrition to infants who simply could not breastfeed. Without this alternative, many infants turned ill or did not survive. While in the hospital, I did encounter a low supply of breastmilk, but instead of opting for formula, I decided to use the donor breast milk that my hospital provided. This is how, in my eyes anyway, it helped me to keep up with my plan for exclusive breastmilk feedings.

Many have looked at donor milk as something unhealthy or nasty; however, it is important to know that there could be nothing further from the truth as long as it has come from a reputable distributor. To learn more about donor breastmilk, I took on the opportunity to serve as a volunteer at a milk bank in my home state. I learned all about how it is filtered, stored, and prepared for patient use. Although this chapter is dedicated to formula feeding, the takeaway from mentioning donor milk is the importance of researching things that you are unsure of so that you may make informed choices for your baby.

Donor breastmilk can also be an option when dealing with formula shortages and recalls. In 2020, we thought COVID-19 was bad, but would anyone have thought that just two years later we would experience a shortage of formula here in the United States? I know I didn't. Social media was a great help in sharing information when the formula was located, and some even went as far as purchasing it for others who may not have been able to reach it in time. These times of crisis helped us bond with one another and do what was best for the survival of the baby. If your hospital offers donor breastmilk, look into using it. It can help you reach your exclusive breastmilk goals while your body works to produce a greater milk supply, and if you are planning to breastfeed and bottle feed, it is a great way to save your formula bottles.

If you walk down the aisle of your local Target, Walmart, or any other retailer that sells formula, you will also find that formula also comes in different formulations. There are ready-to-feed options, which are bottles that do not need to be mixed or warmed for the infant. Just attach an appropriately sized bottle nipple and feed. There are also powdered-based formulas that require the adult to follow instructions to mix with sterile or distilled water before feeding. Whether you choose the powdered or ready-to-feed version of the formula, or even deeper, regular, sensitive, or organic within these variations, they all come with a heavy price tag. If you receive gift cards as gifts and are planning to formula feed, it would be a good idea to use them on formula purchases.

As with breastfeeding, formula feeding comes with its own unique set of challenges. No matter which method you choose, the goal is a healthy, happy baby. To have a healthy, happy baby, you also need to have happy and healthy parents. Trust your instincts. Do your research. Come up with a feeding plan that best suits your lifestyle and what works best for you. Just please know your facts so that you can make an informed decision.

CHAPTER 9

CPR

When my best friend was pregnant, I created a to-do list in preparation for her baby girl. One item listed on that to-do list was to take a CPR class. Cardiopulmonary resuscitation is CPR. It is the process of returning oxygenated blood to critical organs, the brain, and the heart. When the letters C-P-R are heard, it is safe to say that many people may immediately associate them with an adult. Infants and children are small humans that may require resuscitative measures as well. When she read about taking a CPR class, like most people, at first glance she said, "WHAT?" AND "WHY?" Because any human being may need CPR at any given point in a person's life, the class teaches you how to perform life-saving measures for adults, infants, and children. It can mean the difference between life and death. The stories that you hear about children putting anything and everything in their mouths are true.

When my son was about four months old, my husband called me and told me that he saw something stuck to the roof of our son's mouth but couldn't tell what it was. He said he hasn't fed him yet because he was afraid that the nipple on the bottle would loosen it and possibly cause it to be swallowed. Luckily, this was an early work day for me, and I was in route home. When I arrived, I had to take off my mom hat to not freak out and put on my nurse hat to figure out what it was and how to remove it. It turned out to be a wiggle eye. What is that you say? For my non-crafty readers, it is a craft item used to make eyes on picture drawings. I was so proud of my husband for thinking safety first and not feeding him. CPR measures may have been needed and were gladly avoided. My husband was not certified at the time, but I could see from the relief on his face when I retrieved the wiggle eye that he was glad that I was there in case we needed it. He has since become certified in CPR.

As a nurse and a parent, my first concern for my child is their safety. While I also questioned his daycare about why this item was within his reach, a situation like this could have also happened at home. CPR is an essential tool needed in your toolbox to maintain your baby's safety. It is highly encouraged to sign up for the training. You never know when these skills may be needed. Many hospitals will host CPR classes for expectant parents. Once you know the hospital that will be delivering your baby, be sure to ask about any classes that they offer. Additionally, they are often free to you as a registered patient. If your hospital doesn't, try going to the American Heart Association's website to locate a class in your local area.

A common saying for childrearing is "It takes a village." It is encouraged to have that village become CPR-certified as well. Better yet, anyone who will be trusted to care for your newborn should undergo CPR training. Consider making it a group event where everyone attends the class and learns together. It is a great bonding activity for the family as well as an easy way to eliminate the what-ifs that come when you are unprepared for emergencies. There are so many full hearts and love awaiting your little one. Show that love for this baby begins with the *heart*!

CHAPTER 10

SAFE REGISTRY

Registries are typically considered when one is planning for an upcoming baby shower. The experience of completing a registry can be filled with mixed emotions. One in which some people may choose to avoid altogether and opt for a monetary gift in the form of cash or gift cards. If you are one of those who decide to pursue a registry, there are a few things to consider. Is the retail store easily accessible? Are there items that will fit all of your guests' potential budgets? Does the store have an online presence? Does the store provide an option for delivery? Should I have more than one registry? The answers to these questions may help you narrow down which retail store is best for you or if a registry is best for you at all. The good part is that the only right answer is the one that meets YOUR needs.

Did you choose to move forward with the registry? If so, there are a few essentials that are highly recommended.

Highly Recommended		
Diapers	Bottles	
Size newborn	4 ounces	6 ounces
Size 1	8 ounces	10 ounces
Size 2	Pumping bottles	Pumping bags
Diaper cream	Baby wipes	
Swaddling blankets	Burp cloths	
White onesies	Baby bibs	

Other items that are high contenders include:

High Contenders	
Pacifiers	Hats
Hand mittens	Clothing
Socks	Rattles
Teething rings	Crib bedding

Now I know you are probably thinking, "What about the other stuff?" Well, were you thinking about the crib, bassinet, or even a pack in play? You are correct; these are items that one may add to a registry; however, I have found that oftentimes, grandparents, the best friend, or even the parents themselves may have already purchased the higher-ticket items. The items that I listed above are the essential items that will make the biggest difference during those first few weeks. Upon the baby's arrival, as new parents, you will be able to gain a sense of the items needed for your baby. Otherwise, you can run into the possibility of a nursery full of *stuff* that you will never need or use, for that matter. So, what about stuffed animals, you may ask? This item is a hard NO for me. The reason is that they are a safe sleep hazard for a newborn infant. Advertisements, TV, and movies may portray infants sleeping on the bed with a stuffed animal as a cute and comforting element; however, due to the risk of suffocation, this is completely unsafe. For safe sleep, a newborn should sleep alone on their back and in their cribs until they have reached 1 year of age. If you have stuffed animals, please be sure to keep them away from your newborn when sleeping, and this includes naps as well.

Other items that are marketed toward new parents are items that help babies feel comfortable, like they are still in the womb. Let's think about this one. If a newborn has been deemed able to be discharged from a hospital to start their life in their new home outside of the womb, why do they need to feel like they are *in* a womb? The goal is for the baby to feel comforted, safe, and loved in your presence. This is the time to use the one thing you can't buy, YOU! You will be amazed at how skin-to-skin, singing, talking, and holding your baby will give them everything they need to feel comforted, safe, and loved. No store has those values in stock. Only you do!

Are you choosing not to have a registry? This option, too, has its pros and cons. A pro is that you have bypassed that day or two spent scanning items to add to your registry. The con is that you have to go and purchase everything yourself. The more I think about it, it's not a con. I mean, if you are already there to scan the item, you could go ahead and purchase it and save yourself the trip. Another con could be if the gift card is generic, like a Visa or Mastercard, withstanding the urge not to spend the money elsewhere. Asking for gift cards at a specific location may help you stay focused on why you requested them.

No matter which way you choose, the decision should be based on YOUR family's needs and what is best for YOU!

CHAPTER 11

CAR SEATS

Driving home from the hospital can be both an exciting and scary time. It is a transitional period where you are leaving twenty-four hours of monitoring for the birthing person and baby and leaving with this little life to care for while continuing to recover from the birth. One essential item needed for travel is the car seat. I can recall when I was pregnant with my son, my husband and I were so excited to start our registry and get all the baby gear. When it came to deciding on a car seat, we had no clue where to start. As an active mother/baby nurse, the one thing I knew for sure was that it had to be safe. Well, what does a safe car seat look like? Shouldn't they all be safe? I mean, they are for babies, right? It may come as a shock to many, but a lot of the products available for purchase for newborns play into the desires of the parents and the fears of every neonatal health care professional because they may not all be truly "safe." For a car seat to be considered "safe," it must meet the Federal Motor Vehicle Safety Standards and should be indicated somewhere on the car seat. If it doesn't, it's a NO for me, and for the sake of your traveling infant, it should be a NO for you too!

An infant who is born prematurely, small for their gestation age, or with a congenital malformation that affects their ability to adequately breathe in certain positions may require what's called a car seat challenge or tolerance testing. If this is ordered by your medical provider, most healthcare facilities will require the use of a car seat that meets the Federal Motor Vehicle Safety Standards and the American Academy of Pediatrics guidelines. According to the American Academy of Pediatrics Policy Statement (2018), five best practice recommendations that support optimal safety for children of all ages during travel include:

1. *"All infants and toddlers should ride in a rear-facing car safety seat as long as possible until they reach the highest weight or height per manufacturer's guidelines."*

2. *"All children who have outgrown the rear-facing weight or height limit for their car safety seat should use a forward-facing car safety seat with a harness for as long as possible, up to the highest weight or height allowed by their manufacturer."*

3. *"All children whose weight or height is above the forward-facing limit for their car safety seat should use a belt-positioning booster seat until the vehicle lap and shoulder seat belt fits properly, typically when they have reached four feet, nine inches in height and are between eight and twelve years of age."*

4. *"When children are old enough and large enough to use the vehicle seat belt alone, they should always use lap and shoulder seat belts for optimal protection."*

5. *"All children younger than thirteen years should be restrained in the rear seats of vehicles for optimal protection."*

When planning for the arrival of your newborn, prematurity or any birth-related issues most often don't come to mind. Life is always life "ing" so as a rule of thumb, ensure your car seat meets the safety standards.

CHAPTER 12

ADVOCACY

Many of us don't know the power of our voices. This is especially true in healthcare. When you are unaware of the meaning of medical terms being used by your provider or nurse, ask them to explain their meaning. If you are told that you need a procedure or a certain course of treatment, ask why. What are the benefits versus the risks? You have the right to know and work with your medical team instead of simply following orders about your health. To be clear, your provider is your expert, and I am in no way saying to go against their advice. What I am saying is that you have a right to know how and why this decision is being made for your care. Most providers are open to a patient- and family-centered model of care and will take the time to ensure that your questions have

ADVOCACY

been answered and you understand the plan. If they do not, RUN! It's time to find a new provider who is willing to explain but, more importantly, to listen. No one knows your body better than you do. Your knowledge about you is invaluable and plays a major role in your plan of care.

Some voices may need to be helped to be heard through interpretation services. It is a requirement by law to have a means for patients whose first language is not English or who are deaf. I have had patients refuse this service. It is highly encouraged to use them, even if you don't feel that you need them. It provides a second line of communication to ensure that what you say is translated the way that it was intended. It is discouraged to use family members. One reason is that, due to some cultural stipulations, they may not reveal everything that was said back to the provider or back to the patient. This can be detrimental to the next steps in your care plan.

When caring for deaf patients, I have been told, "I don't need an interpreter. I can read lips." COVID-19 sent lip-reading out the window. Although a mask is not required any longer, there are still reasons to use one in a hospital, and having this service readily available is of the utmost importance. Not to mention, once again, that it ensures that not only do you understand what the nurse or provider is saying, but your medical team understands you as well. I once told a colleague that due to the rates of maternal morbidity and mortality, I felt like everyone needs someone knowledgeable in every field, especially healthcare, to speak up on the patient's behalf. Since then, I have learned even more that the real power comes from the voices of the patient on their behalf. Advocate for yourself. Use your voice. No one knows you like you!

CHAPTER 13

YOU'VE DELIVERED! HOW DO YOU FEEL?

When the baby arrives, it is one of the most rewarding experiences a couple will ever go through. In most cases, family and friends are so excited and can't wait to meet the new little one. Oftentimes, when family and friends do arrive at the hospital or your home to meet the baby for the first time, the baby is who they are looking to see. How often have you seen the birthing person to be the first one greeted? Some may ask if you are breast- or bottle-feeding. How often does anyone ask if the birthing person has eaten lately? Other questions may include, How is the baby sleeping? How often has any visitor questioned the rest of the birthing person?

Birthing persons are dealing with hormonal changes, an internal outlook on their appearance, and, boy, are they tired. No matter what they say, they are tired. As a mother/baby nurse, I have witnessed just how tired a birthing person and their support person can become. It's as if their bodies are completely drained after the stress of waiting during labor and then the act of delivery. Your adrenaline is at an all-time high, and once your body settles down, it crashes. As tired as we know you are, please know that your nurses understand; however, we still have to conduct assessments, monitor you and your baby, and administer medications. The nurses are simply doing their job, and whenever possible, they will leave you alone to rest. Our job is to make sure that you and your new family are doing well in anticipation of discharge.

The discharge procedure consists of the birthing person taking some form of postpartum depression assessment. Be prepared to receive one of the most common assessments, The Edinburg Postnatal Depression Scale. It is a ten-question screening survey to identify signs of postpartum depression. This is not to judge you. It is to make sure that, based on your responses, you receive the resources that best fit your needs. I have to admit that when I had to complete this assessment myself, I wasn't truthful. I found myself trapped under the stigma that postpartum depression was not something that I could have. I mean, I am a mother/baby nurse after all. How would that look? It would look normal, THAT'S ALL! After opening up to some of my colleagues, I learned that I was not alone in my feelings during the postpartum stage of my pregnancy.

As a nurse in this specialty, it is easy to make yourself believe that you should have this mothering thing down. I mean, we teach new parents how to care for themselves and their newborns every day. Not being top-notch at this never crossed my mind, but I wasn't. I was exhausted after having my son. I was not successful at breastfeeding right off the bat. I even dropped my baby after holding him in his carrier without being strapped in. I felt like a total failure. At the time, we moved four weeks after he was born, and my husband travels for work, leaving me alone a lot of the time with this newborn baby. He would check on me and ask if I was okay. I would reply yes, because what else was I supposed to say? The TRUTH, YOU SHOULD TELL THE TRUTH!!! I remember that for whatever reason, one particular day, this answer must not have sat well with him, and he called my sister and brother-in-law. Shortly after talking to my husband, I heard a knock at the door. It was my brother-in-law who said he was just stopping by. It was the break I needed. He held and played with the baby while I took a shower. Because clutter stresses me out, I even cleaned the kitchen. We then had an adult conversation. It was so nice just having him there to be present in my husband's absence.

Sadly, this day did not fully resolve my feelings or the thoughts that entered my head. I recall riding in the car with my husband and our new baby, and before we could get out of the car to return home, I looked at him and said, "I need to see my doctor because I think I need to be on medication." My thoughts were beginning to scare me. After this, we developed a new plan, especially in his absence. I already overcame the first hurdle, admitting that there was a problem. The second step was to identify the source. It was a cross between being tired and feeling the need to do something more. It is hard for me to relax in general. To remedy this, I developed a schedule for myself. I planned ways to get out of the house during the day. My sister and brother-in-law didn't live that far away, so they visited more or would watch him while I ran an errand. This helped me turn a corner. As it turns out, I didn't need the medication after all. I just needed a plan and some rest.

This situation doesn't always work out this way. Some birthing persons may require medications or therapy. If this is you, it's okay. You are doing what is best for you and your budding family. As new mommies and daddies, I encourage you both to tell the truth when you are asked if you are okay. Know that it is normal and okay to not be okay! Mommies and daddies who are healthcare professionals, especially those in the maternal/newborn field, are not exempt, and that too is okay! This is a new experience. Even if this is your second child, it is still a new experience. If someone asks if there is anything that they can do for you, say YES! Give them a specific job. Let them help you.

While most people are only aware of postpartum depression, there are different stages of postpartum depression. Each stage carries a different level of adaptation, ranging from a diagnosis of baby blues to postpartum psychosis. Baby blues is the lesser, and postpartum psychosis is the rarest but most extreme case. Admitting your true feelings can open doors that allow you to better care for yourself and your baby. To my Christian brothers and sisters, we can't pray away this feeling. I tried. I believe that God provides angels on earth to supply our needs as well. The word says that "faith without works is dead." It's time to move.

We as a society need to do better about caring for the birthing parents after delivery, just as much as we are concerned about the baby. Visits should include them as well, not a rush to the baby. Mommies and daddies, believe me when I tell you that it is okay to not be okay. You have been through a lot. You are allowed to feel how you feel. You deserve to have your voice heard on the matter and gain the help that you need to overcome it. If this becomes you, know that you are not alone and that people want to help.

CHAPTER 14

WAIT! MY BABY IS A DOLL

When I was little, there was a show called The Rugrats. During one of the episodes, one of the characters sang a song that included this lyric, "A baby is a gift, a gift from above. A baby is a gift from above, bove, bove." It is true that babies are a gift. They are the most precious gift that we could ever receive in life. We thank our little ones for bringing that special something into our lives by making sure that their lives have the best beginning.

Now that the groundwork has been laid and preparation has been made to keep you well informed, inspired, and confident about keeping your baby safe and thriving, it is now time to have some fun. I love Pinterest so much; I often wonder how I ever functioned without it. So, of course, I had a Pinterest page dedicated to my baby. Nursery ideas, baby shower themes, matching hospital gowns—you name it. These are the things that are exciting and fun when you think about having a new baby, and no one should miss those moments. One way to help rake in some freebies is to attend a baby expo. Here you can enter raffles and drawings to win items on your wish list, or at least receive samples, and have yet another day dedicated to celebrating you and your bump.

One of the easiest and probably the top items to receive at your baby shower will be clothing. This is both cute and necessary with the amount of changing you may do in one day. You should look forward to showering your baby with those beautiful, soft blankets, outfits, and socks. Smelling that sweet baby smell after a bath and holding them oh so delicately. Your baby needs it all. The important and the unimportant things, because that is life. We have to have a balance of focus and fun. Time to work and time to play. We must keep that in mind right from the beginning. Babies feed off of your vibes. Let's be sure we are putting out what we hope they will receive. Plan the life that you see for your baby and think about ways to make that happen. Will it be college funds or trust funds? Will it be a strong sense of self or instilling a strong work ethic? Will it be teaching them to love themselves and love others despite your differences? Will it be a combination of them all? It's all up to you how you dress it up because your baby *IS* a doll.